Accomplish More with Less: Draw in New Clients, Lift Benefit, and Sparkle Over the Rest.

Mark P. Green

SUCCESS
INNOVATION
VENTURE
CUSTOMER
BUSINESS
TEAMWORK
SALES
PERFORMANCE
TEAM
MARKETING
PLAN
SUPPORT
COMPETITION
OPPORTUNITIES
STRATEGY
IDEAS
GOALS

INTRODUCTION

Quite a long time ago, in the clamoring heart of the city, there carried on with a man named Imprint P. Green. Mark wasn't your ordinary money manager. He had a remarkable vision - one that appeared to be practically mysterious in a world fixated on accomplishing more, having more, and continually pursuing the following huge thing.

Mark had confidential, one he was unable to hold on to impart to the world. It was a mysterious that could change the existences of people and change the destiny of organizations. This mystery was perfectly concealed in his book named, "Accomplish More with Less: Draw in New Clients, Lift Benefit, and Sparkle Over the Rest."

The Beginning of a Thought

Imprint's excursion toward composing this book started with a basic inquiry: "Is there a method for accomplishing more with less?" As a carefully prepared business person, he had experienced endless people and organizations that were never-endingly trapped in the tireless tornado of efficiency, taking a stab at progress however frequently coming up short.

One bright evening, while at the same time tasting his espresso at a corner bistro, Imprint wrote down this inquiry in his scratch pad. The response he looked for wouldn't simply transform him; it would change the existences of numerous others as well.

The Journey for Proficiency

In the initial sections of his book, Imprint shared his own account of looking for proficiency and adequacy. He related his initial days as a striving business visionary, shuffling numerous jobs, and the steady sensation of being extended excessively slender. It was this very battle that lighted his energy for tracking down a superior way.

Imprint's book directed perusers through his own excursion of experimentation, finding what worked and what didn't when it came to accomplishing more with less. He shared the tales of individual business visionaries and pioneers who had effectively smoothed out their activities and flourished simultaneously.

Drawing in New Clients

Mark comprehended that drawing in new clients was really difficult for organizations. His book wasn't simply a hypothetical composition on effectiveness; it was a reasonable manual for getting new customer base.

He recapped the tale of a little pastry kitchen proprietor who executed a portion of his techniques and saw an exceptional expansion in people strolling through. The pastry shop's warm smell and inviting air turned into a magnet for clients who recently passed by without a subsequent look.

Helping Productivity

Benefit was another region where Imprint's book sparkled. He made sense of how a tech startup, near the very edge of insolvency, had turned its fortunes around by rethinking its uses, improving its assets, and zeroing in on what really made a difference. The story filled in as a demonstration of the force of his procedures.

Transcending the Opposition

In the last parts, Imprint shared stories of organizations that had transcended the opposition, not by outspending or outsmarting their adversaries, yet by separating themselves in significant ways. He examined how a little café had figured out how to flourish in an area soaked with large chains by developing a dedicated local area of clients who valued higher expectations no matter what.

Mark P. Green's book wasn't simply a gathering of business standards; it was an assortment of stories that showed the standards in real life. Through these accounts, he illustrated what was conceivable when people and organizations embraced the idea of accomplishing more with less.

The Commitment of Change

As perusers ventured through the book, they regarded themselves as propelled and roused. They understood that Imprint's mystery wasn't sorcery; it was a very much made methodology for progress. The book guaranteed change, for organizations as well as for anybody able to rock the boat and take on a mentality that supported proficiency and viability.

Mark P. Green's "Accomplish More with Less" wasn't simply a book; it was a guide to a more brilliant, more effective, and more fruitful future. It was an account of one man's journey to improve on progress and his faithful conviction that less could without a doubt be more.

Thus, the narrative of Imprint P. Green and his book lived on, an encouraging sign in a world that occasionally appeared to be overpowered by the quest for more. It remained as an update that with the right mentality and procedures, anybody could accomplish their objectives with beauty, straightforwardness, and indeed, less.

9

○ **The Importance of a 1-Page Marketing Plan**

In the current high velocity and consistently propelling business scene, the occupation of displaying has become more essential than any time in late memory. Whether you're a spread out big business, a little startup, or a solitary financial specialist, convincing exhibiting is the spirit of your success. The compass coordinates your picture, the voice that reverberates with your group, and the system that drives your business forward.

In any case, amidst the consistent clatter and competition, the necessity for ease and clarity in advancing orchestrating has never been more central. Enter the 1-Page Advancing Arrangement, a helpful resource expected to cut through the complexity and distil your exhibiting method into a singular, minimized page.

In this time of information over-trouble, the centering skill purchasers are contracting. They're attacked with sees, online diversion updates, messages, and that is only the start. Amidst this surge of messages, associations ought to sort out some way to convey their value quickly and truly. This is where the 1-Page Advancing Arrangement shimmers.

This book is your manual for understanding the significance of a 1-Page Advancing Arrangement and how it can change how you approach displaying for your business. We will research why ease is the way to result in the present advancing scene, how a one-page plan can give fixation and course, and how it will in general be the stimulus for improvement and efficiency.

All through these pages, you'll track down certifiable occasions of associations, both of every kind imaginable, that have outfit the power of a brief elevating plan to achieve excellent results. You'll get comfortable with the little by little course of making your own 1-Page Publicizing Plan, hand crafted to your original targets, group, and resources.

At the point when you show up toward the completion of this book, you'll not simply fathom the meaning of a 1-Page Advancing Arrangement yet furthermore have the data and instruments to create one that can drive your business higher than at any other time. This moment is the best opportunity to embrace straightforwardness in your advancing framework, and this book is your manual for doing precisely that. Could we set out on this journey together and open the ability of your publicizing attempts like never before.

○ **Overview of the Book**

In the high speed universe of business and showcasing, the capacity to distil complex procedures into basic, significant plans is a superpower. "Drafting a 1-Page Showcasing Plan" is your complete manual for saddling the extraordinary capability of a succinct promoting technique.

This book is your fundamental toolbox for exploring the powerful scene of current promoting. We start by underscoring the basic significance of straightforwardness during a time of data over-burden. Intricacy can be deadening, yet effortlessness is engaging. The 1-Page Advertising Plan is your vital aspect for slicing through the commotion and making your message resound.

Our process takes us through the center standards of powerful advertising, beginning with the specialty of characterizing clear business objectives. We dive into the complexities of making a convincing message, picking the right promoting channels, and building a 1-Page Showcasing Plan customized to your special requirements.

Certifiable contextual investigations give significant bits of knowledge, offering a brief look into how organizations of all sizes and enterprises have utilized this way to deal with make surprising progress. You'll gain from their victories as well as from their difficulties, acquiring a more profound comprehension of how to explore the consistently changing promoting scene.

As you progress through the sections, you'll find pragmatic methods for executing your arrangement, estimating results, and investigating normal difficulties that might emerge. We'll investigate systems for scaling your promoting endeavors reasonably, guaranteeing long haul development and brand versatility.

This book isn't simply hypothesis; it's an involved aide. It incorporates formats, worksheets, and assets that enable you to make and refine your 1-Page Advertising Plan as you read. Toward the finish of this excursion, you'll have a vigorous promoting procedure that is compelling as well as versatile to the developing requirements of your business.

In our current reality where consideration is a scant ware and rivalry is wild, the 1-Page Promoting Plan remains as a guide of effortlessness and clearness. Whether you're a carefully prepared advertiser, an entrepreneur, or somebody simply beginning their showcasing venture, this book is your vital aspect for opening the capability of brief, strong promoting systems. Now is the right time to draft your 1-Page Advertising Plan and push your business higher than ever. We should get everything rolling.

CHAPTER 1

● Defining Your Business Goals

At the point when you're simply firing up, it's really smart to lay out objectives for your organization and adjust them to your own objectives also. Consider this guidance for defining objectives that are reasonable for you.

Laying out objectives is a vital piece of picking the business that is ideal for you. All things considered, in the event that your business doesn't meet your own objectives, you most likely won't be cheerful getting up every morning and attempting to make the business a triumph. Sometime, you'll quit investing the energy expected to make the idea work. While laying out objectives, hold back nothing characteristics:

Explicitness. You have a superior possibility accomplishing an objective in the event that it is explicit. "Raising capital" is definitely not a particular objective; "raising $10,000 by July 1" is.

Idealism. Be positive when you put forth your objectives. "Having the option to cover the bills" isn't precisely a rousing objective. "Accomplishing monetary security" states your objective in a more sure way, subsequently starting up your energy to achieve it.

Authenticity. On the off chance that you put forth an objective to procure $100,000 every month when you've never acquired that much in a year, that objective is ridiculous. Start with little advances, like expanding your month to month pay by 25%. When your most memorable objective is met, you can go after bigger ones.

Short and long haul. Momentary objectives are feasible in a time of weeks to a year. Long haul objectives can be for five, 10 or even 20 years; they ought to be significantly more prominent than momentary objectives yet ought to in any case be sensible.

There are a many rudiments to consider while putting forth objects Pay. multitudinous business visionaries start a new business to negotiate financial security. Consider how important cash you need to make during your most memorable time of exertion and every time from that point, as long as five times. Way of life. This incorporates regions like trip, long ages of work, adventure of individual coffers and geographic area. Might it be said that you'll make a trip astronomically or to move? How long would you say you'll work? Which coffers would you say you'll risk? Kind of work. While laying out objects for kind of work, you want to decide if you like working outdoors, in an office, with PCs, on the telephone, with loads of individualities, with kiddies,etc.

Self image delight. Face it: Many individuals start a new business to fulfill their self images.

Possessing a business can be very self image satisfying, particularly in the event that you're in a business that is thought of as impressive or energizing. You want to conclude how significant self image delight is to you and what business best fills that need.

The main rule of self-assessment and objective setting is genuineness. Starting a new business with your eyes totally open about your assets and shortcomings, your preferences and your definitive objectives allows you to defy the choices you'll look with more noteworthy certainty and a more noteworthy likelihood of coming out on top.

With regards to business, there are a ton of elements that can add to a group's prosperity. Nonetheless, quite possibly of the main thing that you can do as a pioneer is to defined clear objectives and goals for your group. This will assist with guaranteeing that everybody is in total agreement and pursuing similar goals.

The following are a couple of ways to define clear objectives and goals:

1. Be Explicit About What You Maintain that Should Accomplish.

2. Ensure Your Objectives Are Sensible.

It's essential to put forth objectives that are attainable. Assuming you put forth objectives that are too high, your group is probably going to get disappointed and surrender. Then again, assuming you put forth objectives that are too low, your group will become careless and may not invest the energy expected to accomplish them.

3.Give Your Group A Course of events.

To keep your group zeroed in and on target, it means a lot to give them a timetable for accomplishing the objectives and goals. This will assist with guaranteeing that they are making a move and gaining ground.

4. Consider Your Group Responsible.

It's vital to consider your group responsible for gathering the objectives and goals. This implies giving ordinary criticism and monitoring their advancement. In the event that they are not gathering the objectives, you might have to change the objectives or offer extra help.

5. Observe Triumphs.

At last, praising victories en route is significant. This will assist with keeping your group spurred and zeroed in on the job that needs to be done.

At the point when they see that their persistent effort is paying off, they will be bound to keep investing the energy expected to accomplish the objectives.

Putting forth clear objectives and targets - How might you ensure your business group is effective

The way to progress for your new companies send off crusade is laying out clear objectives and targets. Without an obviously characterized objective or set of targets, estimating the progress of the campaign unimaginable. With an objective or set of targets as a primary concern, you can tailor your mission to guarantee it arrives at its ideal result.

While defining objectives and targets for your send off crusade, its critical to be practical. Try not to lay out objectives that are too large or excessively little. Plan to accomplish something testing yet feasible. Consider the assets you have accessible and how long you need to finish the mission. Its additionally critical to consider how much cash you can distribute to the mission and whether you will depend on any outsider administrations or programming.

While putting forth objectives, ponder what is generally vital to your organization and how you might want to utilize the send off to accomplish it. For instance, to increment brand perceivability, you might define an objective of arriving at a specific number of individuals inside a certain time period. If you have any desire to increment deals, you might put forth an objective of arriving at a specific income focus inside a certain time span.

As well as laying out clear objectives, setting clear goals for your campaign significant. Targets are more unambiguous than objectives and ought to give further knowledge into how you will gauge achievement. Goals ought to be Savvy: explicit, quantifiable, feasible, pertinent, and time-bound. They ought to likewise be significant: they should spread out what steps should have been taken in other to arrive at the objective.

For instance, on the off chance that you want to increment brand perceivability, your goal may be Contact 100,000 individuals via web-based entertainment in no less than 90 days through designated advertisements. This goal is explicit (100,000 individuals), quantifiable (through designated promotion following), feasible (on the off chance that you have the spending plan), significant (virtual entertainment is one of the most outstanding ways of contacting an enormous crowd), time-bound (90 days), and noteworthy (you understand what should be finished to arrive at this objective).

When you have obviously characterized objectives and targets for your send off crusade, now is the right time to begin arranging and executing the mission. Ensure that all individuals from the group know about the objectives and targets so everybody is in total agreement and making progress toward a similar result. Monitor progress all through the mission so you can change likewise if vital and assess execution toward the finish of the mission to acquire knowledge into what functioned admirably and what could be refined for future missions.

Laying out clear objectives and goals is fundamental for any effective send off crusade, as it permits groups to pursue a typical reason and measure results precisely to illuminate future missions. Taking the time forthright to characterize objectives and targets will take care of over the long haul by guaranteeing that missions are pretty much as successful as conceivable in accomplishing their ideal results.

    ○ **Identifying Your Target Audience**

Envision you're in a bows and arrows challenge while blindfolded. How probably would you say you are to hit your objective — or any objective? Clearly, you'd be probably not going to succeed, and any precision would be blind karma. Like toxophilism, showcasing requires a reasonable view and a firm comprehension of your objective. As such, you want to realize who will probably purchase your items and administrations.

We'll make sense of why pinpointing your image's interest group is vital to your showcasing plan and assist you with distinguishing likely purchasers so you can restrict your advertising effort, associate with your ideal interest group and increment deals.

What is an objective market, and for what reason is it significant?

Each item or administration requests to a particular purchaser type. For instance, expecting guardians and parental figures would be keen on purchasing baby vehicle seats, and well off, style centered individuals would be really willing and ready to purchase fashioner clothing.

An item or administration's potential client should have the accompanying:

A requirement for the item (it should take care of an issue for them, whether or not they're mindful of it)

A longing for the item once they're mindful of it

The monetary capacity to get it

An item might have more than one objective market. For instance, Lego toys have two unmistakable objective business sectors: guardians of rudimentary and center younger students, and Lego-devotee grown-ups who like to assemble things.

Here are only a couple of the ways distinguishing your objective market can help your business:

Centers your promoting financial plan: First, recognizing your objective market assists you with zeroing in your showcasing dollars on arriving at a particular kind of individual so you're not taking an expansive, scattershot methodology. Limiting your promoting center makes your showcasing techniques more compelling, and you squander less cash on attempting to contact individuals who won't ever be keen on the thing you're selling.

Yields improved drives: Promoting to your objective market will bring about more excellent leads and expanded deals since you'll contact individuals with the need, want and capacity to purchase your item.

Assists you with examining your outcomes: Since you're focusing on a restricted crowd, you can concentrate on investigating your showcasing results, contrasting information examination and different promoting components with A/B testing, and making enhancements.

Assists you with fitting your message: One more huge advantage of designated promoting is that it permits you to fit your advertising message explicitly to the client's necessities. For instance, suppose you have a vehicle sales center. While showcasing to more youthful purchasers, you can feature speed, engaging quality and natural highlights. Nonetheless, with more established purchasers, you could zero in on extravagance models and security highlights.

Did You Be aware?

In the wake of distinguishing an interest group, entrepreneurs and promoting groups can design more viable computerized showcasing techniques and showcasing efforts.

Step by step instructions to recognize your objective market

Recognizing your interest group includes making profiles of your optimal clients. These client personas portray who needs your items and administrations so you can market to these clients better. Consider the accompanying strides for distinguishing your objective market.

1. List the characteristics of your interest group corresponding to your item.

List the characteristics of individuals who are probably going to profit from your item. For instance, say you offer a saturating cream. Thin your concentration by recognizing the qualities of individuals your item would interest. For instance, pose these inquiries:

Is it safe to say that they are more youthful or more seasoned?

What advantages would they say they are searching for — comfort, viability, moderateness or hostile to maturing properties?

Could they utilize this item consistently, occasionally or simply on exceptional events?

Conceptualize however many credits as could be allowed to pinpoint explicit client attributes that fit with the item's advantages.

2. Pose inquiries about the socioeconomics and psychographics of your interest group.

While you're distinguishing your crowd, dive profound into socioeconomics and psychographics.

Assemble segment data.

While you're gathering segment data, begin with the self-evident and afterward get more point by point. For instance, pose these inquiries:

Who is probably going to purchase my item?

How old would they say they are?

Could it be said that they are hitched?

Do they have youngsters? How old are the youngsters?

Where do they reside?

What are their pay and instructive levels?

This data will let you know what media to use to contact them and how to speak to them on a basic level. For instance, in the event that you have a home administrations organization, as air conditioning fix, it would check out to zero in on neighborhood promoting techniques to arrive at neighboring mortgage holders and organizations. While you're showcasing to individuals ages 15 to 35, consider utilizing instant message advertising.

Socioeconomics will likewise impact the most convincing pictures for virtual entertainment missions and promotions. For instance, assuming your objective market is hitched couples with kids, use photographs of families. On the off chance that your objective market is youthful, use pictures of more youthful individuals.

Add psychographic data.

Notwithstanding segment data, layer in psychographic data, which offers understanding into why clients could purchase your item or comparable items. For instance, say a theoretical craftsman needs to figure out promising imminent purchasers. A segment and psychographic profile for this sort of craftsmanship purchaser might seem to be this:

Segment:

Ages 40 to 65

Pay $100K+

Schooling: Four year certification or more

Psychographic:

Appreciates engaging at home

Business visionary

Status-cognizant

Aesthetic sciences foundation

Hoping to find and turn into a supporter for new specialists

Each answer ought to bring up new issues, until you have a smart thought of who is purchasing your item

Before you can start to offer your item or administration to any other individual, you need to sell yourself on it. This is particularly significant when your item or administration is like people around you. Not many organizations are stand-out. Simply check out you: What number of dress retailers, home improvement shops, cooling installers and electrical technicians are really one of a kind?

The way to powerful selling in this present circumstance promoting and showcasing experts call a "one of a kind selling recommendation" (USP). Except if you can pinpoint what makes your business special in a universe of homogeneous contenders, you can't focus on your deals endeavors effectively.

Pinpointing your USP requires some hard soul-looking and imagination. One method for beginning is to dissect the way in which different organizations utilize their USPs for their potential benefit. This requires cautious investigation of other organizations' advertisements and promoting messages. In the event that you break down what they say they sell, in addition to their item or administration qualities, you can become familiar with an extraordinary arrangement about how organizations separate themselves from contenders.

For instance, the late Charles Revson, pioneer behind Revlon, consistently used to say he sold trust, not cosmetics. A few carriers sell cordial help, while others sell on-time administration. Neiman Marcus sells extravagance, while Wal-Store sells deals.

Each of these is an illustration of an organization that has tracked down a USP "stake" on which to hang its promoting procedure. A business can fix its USP on item qualities, cost structure, situation system (area and dispersion) or limited time technique. These are what advertisers call the "four P's" of showcasing. They are controlled to give a business a market position that separates it from the opposition.

Some of the time an organization centers around one specific "stake," which likewise drives the methodology in different regions. An exemplary model is Hanes L'Eggs hosiery. Back in a period when hosiery was sold essentially in retail chains, Hanes opened another appropriation channel for hosiery deals. The thought: Since hosiery was a shopper staple, why not sell it where different staples were sold - - in supermarkets?

That position system then, at that point, drove the organization's determination of item bundling (a plastic egg) so the pantyhose didn't appear to be incongruent in the store. Also, in light of the fact that the item didn't need to be squeezed and enveloped by tissue and boxes, it very well may be evaluated lower than different brands.

This is the way to uncover your USP and use it to control up your deals:

Put yourself in your client's shoes.

Too frequently, business visionaries become hopelessly enamored with their item or administration and fail to remember that it is the client's requirements, not their own, that they should fulfill. Move away from your day to day tasks and cautiously examine what your clients truly care about. Assume you own a pizza parlor. Without a doubt, clients come into your pizza place for food. In any case, is food all they need? What could compel them return over and over and disregard your opposition? The response may be quality, comfort, dependability, amicability, tidiness, graciousness or client assistance.

Keep in mind, cost is never the main explanation individuals purchase. Assuming your opposition is beating you on estimating on the grounds that they are bigger, you need to find another deals include that tends to the client's necessities and afterward assemble your deals and special endeavors around that component.

Realize what rouses your clients' way of behaving and purchasing decisions.
 Effective promoting expects you to be a novice clinician. You really want to understand what drives and persuades clients. Go past the customary client socioeconomics, for example, age, orientation, race, pay and geographic area, that most organizations gather to examine their deals patterns. For our pizzeria model, it isn't sufficient to realize that 75% of your clients are in the 18-to-25 age range. You want to take a gander at their thought processes in purchasing pizza - - taste, peer tension, comfort, etc.

Beauty care products and alcohol organizations are extraordinary instances of ventures that know the worth of mentally situated advancement. Individuals purchase these items in light of their cravings (for pretty ladies, extravagance, style, etc), not on their requirements.

Reveal the genuine reasons clients purchase your item rather than a competitor's.

As your business develops, you'll have the option to request your best source from data: your clients. For instance, the pizza business person could ask them for what good reason they like his pizza over others, in addition to request them to rate the significance from the highlights he offers, like taste, size, fixings, climate and administration. You will be astounded the way that legitimate individuals are the point at which you ask how you can work on your administration.

Since your business is simply beginning, you will not have a great deal of clients to ask yet, so "shop" your opposition all things considered. Numerous retailers regularly drop into their rivals' stores to see what and how they are selling. On the off chance that you are truly bold, take a stab at requesting a couple from the clients after they leave the premises what they like and aversion about the contenders' items and administrations.

Whenever you have gone through this three-step market insight process, you want to take the following - - and hardest - - step: getting your psyche free from any assumptions about your item or administration and being mercilessly genuine. What highlights of your business leap out at you as something that separates you? What could you at any point advance that will make clients need to disparage your business? How might you situate your business to feature your USP?

Try not to get deterred. Effective business proprietorship isn't tied in with having a novel item or administration; it's tied in with making your item stick out - - even in a market loaded up with comparative things.

CHAPTER 2

- **Crafting Your Message**

It isn't is to be expected that we pursue the majority of our choices in light of feelings. Once in a while, we use rationale, yet that is simply not the way in which human instinct works. While fostering a computerized promoting technique, we can utilize this for our potential benefit by creating messages that relate to your main interest group's perspective and urge them to choose to make a move in light of feeling. Utilizing sympathy to address that feeling makes the message much more remarkable. I've separated how to assemble the data you really want to create a message that will prevail upon your interest group and make them into clients.

Stage 1: Realize What Your Opposition isn't Realizing.

Your clients are your clients for an explanation, and there are most likely similitudes in their reasons regarding the reason why they picked you. A magnificent spot to begin that learning is to get some information about the feeling they felt that made them in that made them need you. Finding out about your client's close to home reaction when they settled on your business rather than your rival will give you understanding into what your opposition isn't offering what you are. On the off chance that you would like more data on the most proficient method to do this, I as of late composed an article about the most ideal ways to recognize your objective market. In that article, I expound on the best way to recognize likenesses and, specifically, their perspective when they buy your item.

I need to underline that need and close to home responses are two distinct ideas. On the off chance that you are searching for a separation lawyer, you want a separation. Notwithstanding, every individual that needs a separation lawyer has a perspective that drives them to that choice.

The choice to pick one lawyer over another relies upon which best identifies with their feelings. Then again, your client may not "need" your item, for instance, a Rolex watch. There's no earnestness. Be that as it may, there is a status and maybe dramatic skill, among others.

The important point is you want to comprehend what is going through their brains. What feeling will have them make a move? The most effective way to do that is to meet with clients who have previously bought your item or administration. Kindly don't get hung up on actual characteristics like orientation, age, and so on, however plunge further into what's happening in their minds. What was their inclination when they made the buy and grasped the item? What did they feel when they left your office? You can utilize these feelings to begin to create a message that will draw in other people who need to feel the same way.

Stage 2: Get out Whatever Your Opposition isn't Saying

In the event that you and your opposition are saying exactly the same thing, it turns into a contest of who can yell stronger. No business can be everything to all individuals. Despite the fact that they might say, do they really exhibit it? Where does their informing not line up with their execution? It's in these misalignments that you can exploit and where you really want to begin making your message. For instance, suppose you're selling bicycles.

Amazon, Walmart, and Focus on all sell bicycles. You do as well. They presumably sell similar models like you and maybe a couple of dollars less expensive too. How can you contend with organizations that spend more cash publicizing in multi week than you make in a year? You express out loud whatever they aren't saying. Where do you succeed? What might you at any point offer that they can't?

Stage 3: Do What Your Opposition isn't Doing

Indeed, even an organization like Amazon has regions you can take advantage of. For instance, in the event that you have an actual place where a client can contact, attempt, and bring back home across the board visit, you enjoy an upper hand over Amazon. Ponder this. Best Purchase is as yet getting along admirably, even with an Amazon ruled market. You can do likewise.

Your opposition might have cornered the market, however no business can be everything to all individuals, as I said previously. Some succeed in cost and some in client care. Apple is an incredible illustration of individuals paying a premium for what are item gadgets. They utilized feeling to foster a faithful following, and it made their organization one of the biggest on the planet.

As I composed before, in the event that you and your opposition are saying exactly the same thing, it turns into a rivalry to yell stronger. It might be ideal assuming that you offered something else. How about we return to our instance of selling bicycles.

The large box stores sell bicycles. You can go in, get it off the rack, wheel it through the store, pay for it with a few milk and Pop-Tarts, and push it into the rear of your vehicle to bring it home. There is such a lot of that you can do to convey a superior shopping experience. The equivalent goes for a help business. You can do things any other way and maybe more really. Take, for instance, a separation lawyer?

Each separation is unique. Certain individuals need to take advantage of their companions. Then again, there are a lot of couples who would rather not take advantage of their life partner. These couples need a total separation. It's tied in with tracking down that specialty and taking advantage of it.

Last Contemplations

In making the right message, you want to do a tad of schoolwork. You really want to explore your clients and your opposition. Here is a tip: make a calculation sheet, and at the top in the sections, list your rivals. In the left section, make things that your opposition does. You need to make a note, for instance, situating explanation, slogan, administrations, promotion positions, and web-based entertainment openness. At the point when you do this, you can see everything simultaneously, and you can likewise see where you can take advantage of the holes in their informing.

You might discover that they aren't exceptionally dynamic via web-based entertainment or essentially center around cost. Perhaps they center around both cost and client assistance. Try not to go into creating a message pell mell and hurling a lot of poo the wall and seeing what sticks. You have an arrangement to take advantage of where they are powerless. I think I've said it two times as of now, however it is worth focusing on it once more, no business can be everything to all individuals, yet I need to add that in the event that they attempt to be everything to all individuals, they will fall flat at certain things, and that is where you can win!

- ○ **Creating a Compelling Value Proposition**

Making convincing incentives for clients is an essential part of compelling showcasing and business system. An incentive is an unmistakable and enticing explanation that conveys the novel advantages and worth an item, administration, or brand offers to its objective clients. Here are a few critical components and contemplations for creating convincing offers:

1. Client Driven Approach: The incentive ought to zero in on tending to the particular requirements, issues, or wants of the objective clients. Understanding the interest group and their problem areas is pivotal in fitting the offer to impact them.

2. Separation: Feature what separates your item or administration from contenders. Recognize and underline the novel selling focuses and

upper hands that make your contribution stick out.

3. Clear and Compact Informing: The offer ought to be concise and straightforward. Keep away from language and specialized language, ensuring that the advantages are imparted such that any client can get a handle on rapidly.

4. Particularity and Substantial quality: Utilize concrete and explicit language to depict the advantages and results clients can anticipate.

Evaluate results, if conceivable, to add validity and make the offer more unmistakable.

5. Near and dear Charm: Appeal to clients' sentiments and wants. Keeping an eye on functional necessities also as sentiments can make the impetus truly persuading and important.

6. Tackle Issues: Position your commitment as a response for an issue or a strategy for fulfilling a desire. Show how it works on the client's life, easier, or seriously enchanting.

7. Recognitions and Social Check: Including client accolades or evidence of productive use cases can add acceptability and develop trust in the motivation.

8. Consistency Across Channels: Assurance that the impetus is dependable across all promoting and correspondence channels. A bound together message upholds brand character and client wisdom.

9. Perpetual Improvement: Tirelessly survey and refine the motivator considering client analysis and market changes. An effective proposition should progress and conform to stay relevant and persuading.

10. Significance to the Goal Market: Creator the proposal to different client segments if fundamental. Different client get-togethers could have changing necessities and requirements, so the impetus should be appropriate to each part.

Delineation of a Persuading Motivating force:

"Get fit and feel magnificent with our ever-evolving figure out plan that conveys modified works out, ace preparation, and ceaseless progression following. Change your body and achieve your prosperity targets speedier with our verification based approach, maintained by huge number of satisfied clients who have seen bewildering results. Oblige us today and adventure out towards a superior, more cheerful you."

With everything taken into account, making persuading offers incorporates understanding client needs, isolating your commitment, and articulating the benefits in an undeniable, compact, and truly captivating way. A strong proposition can attract and hold clients, drive arrangements, and spread out a high ground keeping watch.

- **Crafting a Memorable Brand Story**

A solid individual brand can separate you from the group and assist you with accomplishing your expert objectives. In any case, to make a successful individual brand, it's vital to create a convincing brand story that catches your one of a kind credits and reverberates with your interest group. In this article, we'll investigate the critical components of an individual brand story and give you noteworthy hints on the most proficient method to make an essential account for your image.

Grasping the Significance of an Individual Brand Story

An individual brand story is something other than a showcasing instrument - it's a strong method for laying out your validity, construct your standing, and interface with your crowd on a more profound level. By making an unmistakable, bona fide brand story, you can separate yourself from your rivals and make an enduring impact on your clients and clients. A very much created brand story can likewise assist you with remaining consistent with your qualities, impart your main goal, and rouse others to make a move.

Be that as it may, what's the significance here to have an individual brand story? At its center, an individual brand story is the one of a kind story that characterizes what your identity is, a big motivator for you, and why you do what you do. It's the story that you enlighten the world concerning yourself, your business, and your extraordinary offer. An individual brand story can envelop various components, including your experience, your encounters, your accomplishments, your qualities, and your objectives.

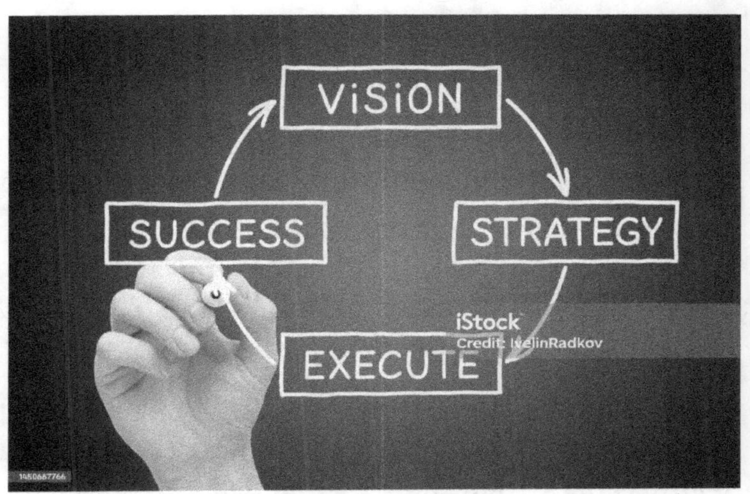

What is an Individual Brand Story?

We should plunge somewhat more profound into what an individual brand story involves. Your own image story is basically your own account - it's an incredible narrative and vocation up until

this point. It's the narrative of how you got to where you are today and what spurs you to continue onward.

While making your own image story, it's critical to consider the vital occasions and encounters that have molded you personally and as an expert. This could incorporate your instructive foundation, your work insight, your own leisure activities and interests, and any difficulties or deterrents you've conquered en route.

However, an individual brand story isn't simply a rundown of achievements or a sequential timetable of your life. It's the tale of your qualities, your interests, and your central goal. It's the tale of why you do what you do and how you have an effect on the planet.

Why Your Own Image Story Matters

Your own image story is the groundwork of your image - it separates you from every other person in your industry and assists you lay out areas of strength for a with your crowd. By sharing your own image story, you can fabricate trust, make a feeling of believability, and draw in your crowd in a significant way.

In the present computerized age, where rivalry is wild and capacities to focus are short, a very much created brand story is a higher priority than any time in recent memory. Your own image story can assist you with hanging out in a packed commercial center and draw in the right clients and clients to your business.

In any case, maybe above all, your own image story can rouse others to make a move. By sharing your own excursion and the examples you've advanced en route, you can persuade others to seek after their own fantasies and have a constructive outcome on the planet.

So set aside some margin to create your own image story- - a useful asset can assist you with accomplishing your objectives and have an effect on the planet.

Distinguishing Your Special Image Ascribes

The most important phase in creating your own image story is to recognize your special image ascribes - the characteristics and attributes that make you particular and noteworthy. This can incorporate many variables, from your abilities and mastery to your character attributes and individual qualities.

While recognizing your novel image ascribes, taking into account both your own and proficient experiences is significant. Ponder the difficulties you've survived, the triumphs you've accomplished, and the examples you've advanced en route. These encounters can assist with forming your image story and make it more engaging to your crowd.

Also, consider the criticism you've gotten from others. Ask associates, companions, and relatives to depict your assets and shortcomings. This can give important experiences into how others see you and how you can use your assets to construct major areas of strength for a brand.

Evaluating Your Assets and Shortcomings

To distinguish your novel image credits, begin by directing a self-evaluation of your assets and shortcomings. Contemplate the abilities and information that put you aside from others in your industry, and consider any regions where you might require improvement. Recognizing your assets and shortcomings can assist you with zeroing in on the components of your own image story that are generally applicable and convincing to your interest group.

While evaluating your assets, think about both hard and delicate abilities. Hard abilities are explicit specialized capacities, like capability in a specific programming or programming language. Delicate abilities, then again, are more theoretical characteristics, like relational abilities, administration capacities, and the capacity to appreciate people at their core.

While evaluating your shortcomings, be straightforward with yourself. Consider regions where you might need insight or information, as well as any private attributes that might be keeping you down. By recognizing your shortcomings, you can do whatever it takes to improve and reinforce your own image.

Characterizing Your Guiding principle

Your guiding principle are the core values that shape your convictions, mentalities, and ways of behaving. Characterizing your basic beliefs can assist you with remaining consistent with your main goal, convey your image message, and fabricate a feeling of validness with your crowd. To recognize your basic beliefs, contemplate the things that are generally vital to you and line up with your business objectives.

While characterizing your basic beliefs, think about both individual and expert qualities. Individual qualities could incorporate things like trustworthiness, uprightness, and empathy, while proficient qualities could incorporate things like advancement, coordinated effort, and client assistance. By distinguishing your guiding principle, you can make an individual brand story that mirrors your bona fide self and reverberates with your main interest group.

Perceiving Your Special Selling Suggestion (USP)

Your remarkable selling suggestion (USP) is the component that separates you from your rivals and goes with you the best decision for your interest group. This can be a particular item or administration highlight, a specific ability or skill, or an extraordinary way to deal with taking care of your clients' concerns. Recognizing your USP can assist you with creating a brand story that features your assets and reverberates with your crowd.

While distinguishing your USP, consider what makes you unique in relation to your rivals. Is it your long periods of involvement with the business? Your imaginative way to deal with critical thinking? Your remarkable client assistance? By understanding your USP, you can make an individual brand story that grandstands your novel assets and separates you from the opposition.

Fostering Your Image Story's Critical Components

Fostering your image story is a fundamental piece of building a fruitful business. Your image story characterizes what your identity is, what you do, and why you make it happen. It is the groundwork of your image character and informing. Whenever you've distinguished your novel image credits, now is the right time to begin creating your image story's key components.

Laying out Your Image's Statement of purpose

Your statement of purpose is the foundation of your image story. The concise assertion characterizes what your identity is, what you do, and why you make it happen. A very much created statement of purpose can assist with directing your business choices, rouse your workers, and draw in clients who share your qualities. To make a convincing statement of purpose, begin by distinguishing your organization's basic beliefs and objectives. Then, distil these into a reasonable and compact explanation that mirrors your image's motivation and vision.

For instance, in the event that your organization is centered around maintainability, your statement of purpose may be a like thing: "To make a more reasonable future by giving eco-accommodating items and advancing mindful utilization."

Making a Convincing Brand Voice and Tone

Your image voice and tone are the manner in which you impart your image message to your crowd. Your voice ought to be predictable across all channels, including your site, online entertainment, and promoting materials. Your tone ought to mirror the qualities and character of your image. Whether your image voice is clever, definitive, or sympathetic, it ought to be an impression of your interesting image credits and resound with your interest group.

While fostering your image voice and tone, consider your crowd and what they esteem. Is it safe to say that they are searching for humor and diversion, or do they favor a more serious and proficient tone? What sort of language and jargon will impact them? By understanding your crowd, you can make a brand voice and tone that will interface with them on a more profound level.

Consolidating Visual Components in Your Image Story

Visual components can assist with rejuvenating your image story and make it more important for your crowd. This can incorporate your logo, variety range, typography, and other plan components that mirror your image's character and style. Consistency is key with regards to visual marking - ensure that your visual components are all firm and mirror your image story.

While planning your visual components, consider the feelings and affiliations you maintain that your image should bring out. What tones and text styles mirror your image's character? What sort of symbolism will resound with your crowd? By making serious areas of strength for a personality, you can help your image stick out and make an enduring impact on your crowd.

By fostering your image story's key components, you can make a convincing and important brand that resounds with your crowd and separates you from the opposition.

Making a Firm and Drawing in Story

Whenever you've laid out the critical components of your image story, now is the ideal time to make a durable and drawing in account that catches your crowd's consideration and has an enduring effect.

Organizing Your Image Story

The construction of your image story ought to be intended to draw in your perusers and fabricate a feeling of expectation and fervor. This can incorporate a convincing opening, a reasonable and convincing outline of your image's main goal and values, and a determination that has an enduring impression. Make sure to keep your image story compact, connecting with, and applicable to your interest group.

Using Narrating Procedures

Narrating is a strong method for interfacing with your crowd on a close to home level and rejuvenate your image story. This can incorporate consolidating individual accounts, client examples of overcoming adversity, or industry measurements. Whatever narrating procedures you pick, ensure that they reverberate with your main interest group and feature your special image credits.

Adjusting Genuineness and Desire

At last, finding some kind of harmony among genuineness and goal in your image story is significant. While it's essential to remain consistent with your qualities and character, it's likewise significant to convey a dream for the future that moves your crowd and separates you from your rivals. By adjusting genuineness and goal in your image story, you can make an account that is both engaging and optimistic for your ideal interest group.

Last Considerations

Creating an important individual brand story is not easy at all, yet it's a critical stage in laying out major areas of strength for a, brand in the present serious commercial center. By distinguishing your extraordinary image credits, fostering your key image components, and making a firm, captivating account that resounds with your ideal interest group, you can make an individual brand story that separates you from the group and assists you with accomplishing your expert objectives.

○ **Developing a Unique Brand Voice**

Your image goes a long ways past your logo and variety conspire. Having a brand voice that reverberates with your interest group is one of the main pieces of building a strong picture and persona that makes clients and clients want more.

Be that as it may, it isn't not difficult to foster a brand voice. Dissimilar to a logo or variety plot, a brand voice is substantially less concrete. It's a continually creating and developing piece of your image, regardless of whether it's something you can't be guaranteed to see.

Your image voice makes you sound human. Yet, past that, it makes consistency among your substance, web-based entertainment channels and the sky is the limit from there. Having an exceptional brand voice can make a conspicuous picture for your crowd, paying little heed to where they're interfacing.

To begin with making your own image voice, the following are four moves toward follow.

1. Depict your image character in only three words.

Before you can make a voice, you want to lay out a personality. This personality ought to be effortlessly characterized and clear to both your representatives and your clients or clients.

Attempt to consider modifiers you might want to depict your image. You could incorporate terms like savvy, accommodating, happy or legitimate.

Consider how your crowd could as of now depict you, or even better, request that they summarize your image in a couple of words. Restricted down your rundown of words to only three that you think best fit the brand you need to assemble.

2. Work out depictions for each word.

Taking the three words you picked in Sync 1, separate portrayals of what they mean to you and your crowd. Make sense of why you picked that modifier and how it affects your organization to show that character attribute. Once more, you need to keep this compact and clear. Attempt to restrict your depiction to only a couple of sentences.

These depictions ought to assist with molding your character, making it simpler for representatives to grasp your image. To shape a durable brand voice, you believe that everybody in your group should comprehend the picture you're attempting to make.

3. Compose do's and don'ts for your image character.

Now that you've distinguished the basic descriptors and depictions for your image character, you can lay out the ways of behaving your group ought to and shouldn't display.

For instance, on the off chance that one of your descriptors is "useful," a "do" may be to respond to questions asked via virtual entertainment rapidly and completely. A "don't" may be utilizing cutout reactions that aren't intended for the client's or alternately client's inquiry.

Separate what ways of behaving you might want to see depict your image character. Your rundown of do's and don'ts ought to make it simple for your workers to depict your image voice in all that they do.

4. Put your new image voice in real life.

Your image voice ought not be a venture you get over to the side when your technique is finished. You want to set it into movement successfully.

To make your image voice steady, it ought to show up in your web-based entertainment posts, on your site and in your other substance. Ensure your scholars comprehend the voice you're attempting to depict and peruse your substance prior to presenting it on guarantee it is on brand.

You ought to likewise habitually revive your image voice. Return to the three words you've chosen, and check whether they actually line up with the picture you're attempting to make. In the event that not, change them out, make another depiction and diagram new do's and don'ts.

What difference does this make?

A brand voice assists you with standing apart from the developing number of brands on the web. At the point when you have an unmistakable and predictable voice that draws in your ideal interest group, you can construct more strong associations that fuel long haul client connections.

While making and keeping a brand voice might appear to be overwhelming, it is definitely worth the work. In the event that you're ready to establish the groundwork for a solid brand character and voice, it will become simpler and more straightforward to develop your picture into something effectively recognizable to your main interest group.

View at your image voice as a unique instrument. Search for new chances to develop and refine your voice, including adding new modifiers to additional drill down the picture you're attempting to depict. Chat with colleagues, workers and clients or clients to hear their thoughts on your character and voice.

At the point when you make something your whole group supports, it will be simpler and more straightforward to make consistency in the voice of your substance.

CHAPTER 3

- **Choosing the Right Marketing Channels**

Not all advancing channels will be great for your business. You really want to do whatever it takes not to consume your time and money by bobbing on board the latest wash channel, which doesn't actually show up at your ideal vested party. So likewise, by then, how might you cultivate a high-impact and down to earth exhibiting system that involves the classy channels for your business?

Everything starts with a system.

For any sort of displaying to be convincing, you maintain that a solid plan should guide you. Looking through in lack of definition isn't the sleek framework for advancing toward anything in business and advancing is plainly no exemption. To assist with imagining your approach and sort out which channels are by and large appropriate for your business, assume about the going with five basics.

1. assume about your articles What are you needing to accomplish out of exhibiting? perhaps you really want to see a development in arrangements of your work and items, raised mindfulness for your picture or further newbies to your handout. Anything that your articles, getting clear on them sets the foundation for your promoting strategy. Each advancing direct studio in an unforeseen manner, and some are lesser at arranging explicit articles than others. For representation, virtual diversion can be an

unprecedented framework for buttressing associations you have with your ongoing client base. A release, likewise once more, could assist with extending mindfulness by getting your picture before piles of eyeballs. Understanding your items suggests you can pick the promoting channels that will help your business the most.

2. Know where you clients hang out

What does your ideal client do on the closures of the week? What kind of media do they consume? What destinations or applications do they a significant part of the time visit and what words could they say they are glancing through on Google?

Buyers are bombarded with media wreck reliably so accepting that your displaying framework will be reasonable, you truly need to know exactly where and when to talk with them. That suggests really trying not to reach them where you accept they ought to be yet rather zeroing in on them where they're presently hanging out.

3. Chat with your customers generally through their outing

We confer to our goal market when they're around the beginning of the channel for clear reasons; we want to encourage them to move to the accompanying time of the purchasing adventure. Anyway, what various associations disregard to do is support these comparable purchasers at whatever point they've changed over.

In case you head out to have a great time with someone and you celebrated the good life, yet they don't hit you up, you end up feeling fairly smoothed and dismissed. This is similarly legitimate for the client relationship. Acquainting assigned illuminating with those clients that have proactively changed over can help you to encourage a more huge relationship with them and empower brand immovability. To grow the advancement of your promoting tries, track down the channels that license you to chat with your buyers pre, during and present arrangement all together on stay related all through the client adventure.

4. Truly investigate the resistance

Need a little course? Perceive your best opponents and note which exhibiting channels they use - a strong characteristic of where you should be planning your undertakings. It confirms that a channel is presumably going to be strong for your business and permits you to get some piece of voice on each channel.

5. Work your framework + separate the results

So you've chosen you goals, found the channels and stages your clients ceaseless and have taken inspiration from you competitors... what next?

You doubtlessly have an exceptionally savvy thought about the exhibiting channels that will end up being savage for your business. Anyway, it doesn't stop there. Displaying isn't set and disregard. It ought to be constantly attempted, improved and revived to stay significant and ensure the best results are achieved. Take advantage of assessment and encounters gadgets that can help with depicting the result of your advancing endeavors. Yet again if you find you're not getting the reaction you had anticipated, change judgment and endeavor.

○ **Exploring Various Marketing Channels**

The present purchasers go to the web because of reasons that go far past basic diversion or an intermittent online entertainment visit with a companion. They're searching for genuine responses and answers for their concerns, including significant data that could end up being useful to them go with more intelligent buying choices.

The term inbound promoting alludes to some strategy that an advertiser could use to draw in new leads, support associations with existing clients, or better address the issues of their ideal crowd. They might achieve this utilizing various channels, including greeting pages, email messages, and websites.

In any case, not all inbound promoting channels are equivalent. A methodology that functions admirably for one brand or industry may not raise a ruckus around town notes for another, so you must pick the most ideal choices. Here is a more critical gander at how to do that.

Excellent Substance in Inbound Showcasing

Nowadays, incredible items and administrations aren't sufficient to catch the consideration of a segregating computerized age crowd genuinely. Fruitful brands likewise comprehend the significance of laying out power, building trust, and supporting long haul connections.

A substance system that spins around really supportive, unique substance is the best approach. The higher the nature of your substance, the more fruitful you'll at the follow:

* Drawing in the right purchasers for your items and administrations

* Successfully captivating your crowd and winning their trust

* Laying out your image as a trustworthy industry authority with genuine answers for offer

* Laying out and holding enduring, commonly advantageous associations with clients

Top 5 Inbound Advertising Channels

As a procedure, inbound showcasing isn't just in sync with what the present purchasers need and anticipate from the brands they pick. It's likewise productive and financially savvy.

Outbound promoting strategies like conventional notices, cold pitches, and mass email can produce leads, as well. Yet, they're not as engaged and can be costly. In the mean time, the typical expense per inbound showcasing lead is about 60% not exactly that related with outbound leads.

Here is a more critical gander at probably the most well known, compelling inbound showcasing channels that effective brands use.

1. Writing for a blog

Keep in mind, fruitful inbound promoting efforts run on extraordinary substance. Google emphatically inclines toward destinations that distribute a lot of it and do so incredibly reliably. Writing for a blog stays one of the best ways of ensuring your image's webpage is one of them.

Supportive, very much enhanced blog entries produce bunches of natural traffic by tending to worries that an interest group could have. Instances of the sorts of posts that function admirably include:

* Top to bottom solutions to normal crowd questions

* Point centered posts about subjects that are mean a lot to your interest group

* Instructions to guides that help individuals with direction, item utilization, and the sky is the limit from there.

2. Web-based entertainment

Like the bigger web, online entertainment has become something beyond a spot to kill a little extra time to a great extent. The present purchasers go there to cultivate connections, with companions and colleagues, yet with brands too.

All things considered, web-based entertainment addresses an invaluable open door that ought to factor into each advertiser's way to deal with inbound showcasing channels. Instances of various ways of utilizing it include:

* Showing ability with high-esteem offers and industry content

* Connecting with your crowd by igniting conversation and partaking in discussions

* Exhibiting new or significant substance from your blog and different channels

3. Email promoting

Email is nearly basically as old as the actual web, and email showcasing has been around close to as long as the bigger universe of advanced publicizing. Notwithstanding, it stays one of the more viable inbound showcasing channels that a brand could utilize.

Not in the least does essentially everybody on the web use email, however a great 99 percent of shoppers actually look at their records everyday. This makes it an incredible method for contacting crowds. Well known strategies include:

* Pamphlets

93

* Selective arrangements and offers

* Overviews and criticism valuable open doors (once in a while with cooperation motivators)

4. Greeting pages

The present buyers answer content that feels individual and is really applicable to them. All things considered, greeting pages can be marvelous ways of driving traffic and convey specific substance to choose crowd subgroups. Instances of ways of utilizing them include:

* Catching lead data

* Boosting activity by offering freemium content

* Empowering email rundown or pamphlet memberships

* Conveying significant area explicit or segment explicit data

5. Podcasting stages

Digital recordings have truly been on the ascent recently. They're one of the most famous inbound showcasing channels and not surprisingly. Like a blog, a digital recording conveys dynamic, continuous substance that makes individuals want more and more. Instances of incredible ways that brands can use podcasting stages include:

* Sending off specialty explicit digital broadcasts that enticement for a crowd of people

* Laying out power and exhibiting aptitude

* Supporting brand character and exhibiting the special character behind your organization

The best choices for you rely completely upon your crowd. Where do they hang out on the web, and how would they get a kick out of the chance to consume data? What picks are the best fit for your image voice and personality?

Amplifying Transformation with Inbound Promoting Channels

Now that you find out about choosing the right inbound showcasing channels, now is the ideal time to take a gander at how you can capitalize on your decisions. Here are a few master tips to remember.

1.Put resources into Search engine optimization

Albeit numerous assets on inbound showcasing list Website design enhancement as a kind of inbound promoting channel, this isn't true. The expression "website streamlining" alludes to an assortment of systems, approaches, and best practices with the possibility to help web search tool perceivability and further develop SERP rankings.

At the end of the day, legitimate Search engine optimization procedures are a fundamental piece of capitalizing on your inbound promoting channels, so you absolutely must put resources into them.

2.Utilize convincing CTAs

Part of completely instructing your crowd on a specific subject is telling them what their following stages ought to be. Solid invitations to take action are a viable method for achieving this. Guide your crowd by telling them what you'd like them to do straightaway, whether it includes concluding a buy, pursuing a mailing rundown, or something totally different.

3.Influence WriterAccess

It requires investment, exertion, skill, and obligation to keep a brand's all's inbound promoting channels appropriately loaded up with top notch content, so you want a dependable, manageable method for re-appropriating different errands. WriterAccess is a top-level, premium commercial center where you can undoubtedly do the accompanying:

* Access huge number of pre-screened, experienced content makers on request

* Influence state of the art matchmaking and content creation devices

* Scale your substance creation endeavors as indicated by your financial plan and needs

* Save yourself a fortune in time, cash, and exertion

* Benefit from the aptitude of new industry voices and qualified specialty specialists.

End

An extraordinary showcasing procedure truly remains closely connected with a painstakingly chosen set of inbound promoting channels that suit your image, crowd, and objectives. In any case, you want genuinely powerful satisfied to get where you need to go.

- ○ **Selecting Channels Aligned with Your Audience**

Picking the right touchpoints and channels for your image procedure is critical for making an essential and predictable brand insight for your clients. In any case, how would you choose which ones to utilize and how to actually coordinate them? In this article, we'll direct you through a few critical stages and tips to assist you with settling on shrewd decisions for your image.

Map your client process and touchpoints.

A client venture is the way that your clients take from becoming mindful of your image to buying, utilizing, and suggesting your items or administrations. A touchpoint is any resource or communication between your image and your clients, like your site, virtual entertainment, bundling, or client support. By planning your client process and touchpoints, you can distinguish the vital minutes and valuable chances to impact your clients' insights, feelings, and ways of behaving. You can likewise recognize any holes or shortcomings in your current touchpoints and channels and further develop them.

Pick your channels in light of your crowd and message.

A channel is the medium or stage that you use to convey your touchpoints, like email, video, blog, or digital recording. Picking the right channels for your image methodology relies upon your crowd and message. You want to comprehend who your clients are, where they invest their energy, what they worth, and how they like to consume data. You additionally need to consider what sort of message you need to pass on, how perplexing or basic it is, the way captivating or useful it is, and how every now and again or reliably you need to impart it. By picking the channels that match your crowd and message, you can advance your scope, significance, and effect.

Incorporate your touchpoints and channels for a consistent brand insight.

While thinking up a brand technique, one of the greatest difficulties is ensuring that touchpoints and channels cooperate flawlessly. You would rather not befuddle or baffle clients with conflicting or inconsistent messages across various touchpoints and channels. All things being equal, endeavor to make a bound together brand experience that builds up your image personality, values, and commitment. To do this, coordinate your touchpoints and channels by utilizing a reliable manner of speaking, style, and character, adjusting your visual components to mark rules, making a reasonable incentive and source of inspiration for each touchpoint and channel, customizing and redoing touchpoints and channels to suit client necessities, inclinations, and input, and testing and upgrading for convenience, execution, and fulfillment.

Assess and adjust your touchpoints and channels in light of information and criticism.

Picking touchpoints and channels for your image methodology is certainly not a one-time choice. A continuous cycle requires consistent assessment and variation in view of information and criticism. You really want to screen and quantify how your touchpoints and channels are performing against your image objectives and targets, utilizing measurements like mindfulness, commitment, transformation, maintenance, steadfastness, and promotion. You likewise need to gather and dissect criticism from your clients, utilizing strategies like studies, surveys, appraisals, remarks, or social tuning in. By assessing and adjusting your touchpoints and channels in light of information and criticism, you can further develop your image system and make a superior brand insight for your clients.

○ **Budget Considerations**

Your C&G coordinator can assist you in creating a budget based on your project's s pecific needs and funding sponsor limits and requirements.

Proposal budgets will vary based on specific project needs and sponsor guidelines. You may wish to consider the following items when planning your proposal budget. Please keep in mind that you must also demonstrate how the budget lines you are requesting will directly support or benefit the work that

you are proposing to the sponsor.

Project personnel and how much effort % project staff should receive for working on

the project.

•This includes the PI.

•Supplies such as consumable scientific •supplies, chemicals, reagents, •antibodies.

•Animal purchases

•Animal care costs

•Core expenses

•Project related travel

•Human subjects incentive payments

•Clinical care costs (if proposing a clinical trial or project which will involve patient care)

•Equipment (Please consult with your C&G coordinator regarding including equipment on proposal budgets)

•Subcontracts (if working with investigators external to UM)

Please keep mind that the following items are typically unallowable on proposal budgets. If you feel that your proposal will require one or more of these, please work with your C and G

Coordinator to see if the particular budget item can be included in the proposal budget:

- Administrative salaries

- Stipends (these are allowable only on a very small subset of awards)

- Hosting costs

- General use items such as office supplies, computers, or items that will be difficult to demonstrate

as only being used for one specific project

It is UM and SoD policy to recover full indirect costs (IDC) whenever possible. UM's current indirect cost rates are as follows:

On Campus Organized Research 56%

Other Sponsored Activity (this covers many clinical trials or projects for which a pre-defined protocol exists) 29%

Off Campus Projects 26%

Notice that the distinction between the different IDC rates is the type of activity being performed, not the source of the funds.

Please consider the IDC rate when planning your proposal budgets. Some funding agencies/organizations present funding limits in terms of total costs which include direct and indirect costs. Faculty can request an IDC waiver which can reduce the IDC rate for your proposal. Contact your C&G coordinator for more details on how to apply for an IDC rate waiver.

CHAPTER 4

- **Building Your 1-Page Marketing Plan**

You can't successfully showcase a business without making a helpful promoting plan. A key guide that is utilized to coordinate, execute, and track showcasing systems over a particular period, a promoting plan fills in as a significant aide for any private company.

Lots of advertising plan frames are accessible on the web, however they are normally expansive, pointless records with unclear headings. It's little marvel, then, at that point, that main 40% of B2C and 37 percent of B2B organizations have one. In any event, when they do, their showcasing plans are generally questionable, excess, awkward, and - more than anything - basically futile.

Enter the one-page promoting methodology: A brief showcasing plan that is reduced to the most significant and noteworthy parts. Laying out one is among the most effective ways to launch and enhance your advertising endeavors.

 The dangers of doing without one are extensive, and they include:

* loads of sat around idly and cash on incapable methods

* vulnerability about why your private venture is participating in showcasing by any means

* an incoherent methodology across media stages, making brand disarray

* conflicting advertising messages that confound and estrange possibilities

* deteriorated development because of muddled and mixed showcasing endeavors

Top Advantages of a One-Page Promoting Plan

A portion of the top benefits of a one-page showcasing plan include:

* gives clearness and bearing to your advertising endeavors

* brings about an outwardly shocking record that gives brief direction

* makes steadfast supporters and "super fans" who become recurrent clients

* gives a more spry approach to promoting an independent company

* keeps you and your group zeroed in on gathering targets all the more without any problem

* can be modified and improved persistently and effortlessly, guaranteeing ideal promoting endeavors

Seven Inquiries to Pose While Laying out a One-Page Showcasing Plan

Pose yourself these seven inquiries while endeavoring to foster a compelling one-page promoting plan:

1. Who is your crowd? - Be explicit. For instance, "men between the ages of 35 and 55" is excessively dubious. All things considered, something like "men ages 35 to 55 who are fathers, heads of family and who have postgraduate educations" works better.

2. What are their interests? - What keeps your interest group up around evening time? What is it that they need to accomplish to determine those concerns? Once more, be explicit. For instance, assuming you sell cosmetics, you're not simply selling beauty care products - you're selling confidence and certainty.

3. Could your organization at any point address their basic necessities? - Utilizing the above model, inquire as to whether your items or administrations can further develop your interest

group's confidence. Articulate your contributions and make sense of how they address the fundamental issue. For example, your cosmetics is intended for explicit appearances, making it quick and simple for individuals to put their best self forward.

4. What is your center showcasing message? - You ought to have the option to depict it in only a couple of sentences.

5. What are your particular advertising objectives? - Be quite certain; incorporate genuine numbers and timetables. For instance, maybe you need to include 500 new supporters virtual entertainment in three weeks or less.

6. What are your key presentation markers? - How might you realize that you have accomplished your objectives? Hold back nothing number inside a characterized period, whether it be the ideal number of site hits, changes, or devotees.

7. What is your advertising activity plan? - How might you accomplish your objectives? Characterize whether you will zero in on something like email promoting messages offering selective arrangements or on paid publicizing on stages like Facebook and Google.

Components to Remember for a One-Page Promoting Plan

While creating your showcasing plan, make certain to incorporate these components:

* Title: Incorporate the name of the item or administration and the period for your technique.

* Item or Administration: Depict the contribution and the advantages that it gives.

* Ideal interest group: Characterize your main interest group in view of sorted through purchaser personas.

* Key Differentiators: Explicitly portray how your item or administration contrasts from others in your specialty.

* Benefits: Framework the essential advantages of your item or administration.

* Client Assessment: Which credits of your interest group matter? For instance, would they say they are essentially situated in a particular topographical district?

* Promoting System: Show a couple of essential showcasing methods and how they will be executed.

* Unique Offers: Will you be offering exceptional estimating or different arrangements as a feature of your promoting plan?

* Imaginative Components: Which components should your promoting group center around? For example, list fundamental catchphrases,

expressions, or themes to remember for showcasing materials.

* Media: Rundown the basic types of media that will shape the premise of your arrangement. For instance, you could refer to paid promoting or online entertainment channels.

* Benefit/Misfortune Projection: Incorporate the assessed benefit or misfortune for the designated items over the characterized advertising period.

* Surveying Results: How might you decide how every client found out about the item or administration? Which stages would they say they were on?

CHAPTER 5

- **Executing Your Plan**

As significant as making a well conceived plan is in accomplishing business objectives, many shops need to move their accentuation to the execution of the arrangement. The execution step is definitely not a glamourous as making a splendid arrangement. Likewise, it requires significantly more exertion. Composing an arrangement may just require a couple of long stretches of conceptualizing. Then again, executing an arrangement is a day to day action. It's where the difficult work truly happens.

Plan Your Work, Work Your Arrangement

Execution is troublesome in light of the fact that it expects everybody to zero in on those exercises that are critical to your system as opposed to respond to the pressing yet not really significant. These dire requests on time frequently become certifiable Chinese fire bores that divert from the organization objective.

As a rule execution demands great time usage abilities. Here are a few abilities you ought to create:

• Start making a day to day "what should be done" list. Many individuals compose their rundown toward the start of the day. What's better is to design the upcoming work toward the finish of the present working day.

• After you have gathered the rundown, focus on your exercises in view of their significance to your organization objectives. Keep away from those irrelevant exercises that sit around idly. These are for the most part exercises that you need to do, yet don't have to do. Generally speaking, you ought to just scratch off any irrelevant errands from your rundown.

You can't do everything. In the event that you don't have the assets to chip away at something, scratch it off of your schedule. Truth be told, you ought to wipe out movements of every sort that don't line up with your objectives.

• At the point when you get to the shop, center around the main undertakings. These are the exercises that line up with your organization's essential objectives and which will deliver the best outcomes. The allurement for the vast majority is to deal with assignments which are the simplest to do. Following through with these responsibilities provide you with a misguided feeling of achievement.

By and large the main assignments are the most troublesome and generally the errands that individuals follow up on last. In the event that conceivable, you ought to designate the less considerable exercises to subordinates.

Assuming you realize your partners well, you know their assets and shortcomings. In light of this, you ought to understand what you can and can't delegate to them.

Assuming you know a partner's shortcoming, you can mentor them to work on their presentation. On the off chance that you know their expert desires, you can guide them as they make progress toward their objectives.

Instructions to Group Felines

In working with groups getting everybody in total agreement is frequently troublesome, particularly while working with imaginative individuals. Concentrating areas of strength for of people resembles crowding felines.

Some vibe that you shouldn't actually attempt. Simply give your felines a task and a cutoff time and allow them to do whatever they might want to do. In the event that you are free ordinarily, a feline as it were, it's difficult to contradict this methodology. That is, assuming you accomplish your desired outcomes.

- ○ **Actionable Steps for Implementation**

An undertaking plan or task execution plan is a key report that keeps groups on target all through a venture, showing how a venture is supposed to run alongside who's liable for what. It's an incredibly significant arranging apparatus — one that can be the distinction between project achievement and undertaking disappointment.

It's likewise a genuinely complete report, and in the event that you've never constructed one, the idea can feel a piece overpowering.

In the present post, we'll give you a five-step plan for building and executing an undertaking plan. To begin with, we'll walk you through what a venture execution plan resembles, why you ought to make one for each task, and what each plan ought to incorporate.

Execution plan: What to incorporate and 5 fundamental stages

What is an undertaking execution plan?

An undertaking execution plan is a record that characterizes how a task will be executed. Execution plans make sense of the essential objectives and steps engaged with a task, characterize the undertaking consummation course of events, and rundown the assets (counting colleagues) important for a fruitful venture.

Project execution plans are some of the time called "smart courses of action" since they spread out the methodology proposed for a task. Yet, we like the more extended name since it conveys something beyond methodology: It proposes an interaction going right into it, and it responds to the subject of how a group will show up at an objective.

Utilizing an undertaking plan is one of a few task the board best practices. It's likewise unique in relation to a work plan: A work plan manages undertakings, time spans, and individual work bundles, while a venture execution plan manages a lot more extensive scope of data.

Why each task ought to begin with an execution plan

Why start each task with an execution plan? Straightforward: on the grounds that you believe the undertaking should succeed, and you believe that a goal way should be aware assuming it succeeded.

Beginning each venture with an execution plan achieves a lot for most groups and organizations, fundamentally on the grounds that it makes a common feeling of vision and understanding and focuses toward a plainly characterized objective.

Most groups understand these four advantages (and bounty more) when they make an intensive and practical task execution plan:

It makes a significant guide of the extent of work

Projects run the range from very easy to extended and complex. The more confounded and interconnected the task, the more prominent the opportunity for disarray.

Anything that the degree of intricacy, mayhem results when colleagues aren't sure about what to do, when to do it, or why they're making it happen.

A task execution plan is the cure to this sort of confusion since it shows all gatherings what the way ahead resembles (the guide) — as well as what is and isn't on that way (the extent of work).

It makes objectives and correspondence straightforward to all partners

At the point when all gatherings comprehend the objectives of an undertaking, you reduce disarray around those objectives. There might in any case be conflict on the most proficient method to best accomplish an objective, however there's no disarray about the thing the group is planning to achieve.

Likewise, a focal, open record containing all important parts of a venture makes a solitary wellspring of truth for groups, chiefs, leaders, merchants, clients, from there, the sky is the limit. At the point when everybody related with a task is working from similar playbook, groups and organizations appreciate more clear, more engaged, and more straightforward correspondence.

It considers your colleagues responsible

Around 70% of organizations report having something like one bombed project somewhat recently. We've all been important for a task where nobody appeared to be responsible for issues or even all out project disappointment. Obviously, nobody likes assuming the fault and it isn't generally horribly useful to track down a substitute. In any case, assuming you have a colleague or specialty unit that is reliably neglecting to convey, you need to be aware.

A solid venture execution plan clarifies who's liable for what inside an undertaking. It gives project directors and group drives a more grounded comprehension of undertaking responsibility, assisting with considering colleagues responsible for their work.

Also, more often than, worse responsibility accompanies improved results!

It assists your whole group with remaining in total agreement

You won't ever totally take out project-related tasks getting out of control (something that happened inside in excess of 33% of activities in

2021), nor would it be a good idea for you. Boundaries for different expectations or even the whole undertaking can and do adjust over the direction of a venture, and some of the time an adjustment of extension is obviously the ideal choice.

Be that as it may, not all tasks running amok is great. Particularly with longer or more perplexing undertakings, it's normal for colleagues to lose center around the high level objectives — also the particular advances expected to arrive at those objectives.

This deficiency of center is preventable, however, just like the tasks running amok that develops from it. An undertaking execution plan keeps the 10,000 foot view objectives and the means expected to meet them in center. At the point when an adjustment of extension is justified, it ought to be reported inside or close by the execution plan.

Fundamental parts of an incredible execution plan

Most very much planned execution plans contain these fundamental things, however it's critical to take note of that execution plans shift generally, very much like the undertakings they're connected to.

These components contain a strong starting point for your next execution plan. Begin with these, however go ahead and add extra components that appear to be legit for your industry or venture type.

Scope articulation

The degree explanation frames the extent of the task — basically, what work will be acted in the venture (and what work would be viewed as out of extension).

Project achievements, objectives, and key goals

Project objectives are the undeniable level results the venture plans to accomplish. Key targets are the means or halfway results that will happen all through the undertaking on the side of the task objectives. Project achievements are the marks of estimation en route, generally critical or unmistakable here and there.

Instances of achievements across a couple of industry settings incorporate wireframe finished, beta send off, duplicate drafted, or the fruition of a stage, fragment, or capability that is important for the entirety.

Itemized asset plan

A task's asset plan shows which HR are involved alongside their time or responsibility. You ought to likewise incorporate materials and hardware (commonly, just what's past the standard stuff each representative as of now has) required for effective task consummation.

Assessed execution course of events

A vital component of any execution plan is a substantial time period for the undertaking (and its execution). These dates are seldom wonderful at the start of a task, however they give an objective to pursue and give partners some setting for what they're approving.

Most task groups use project the executives programming for making project timetables, frequently as a Gantt graph.

Execution plan achievements

Your execution plan might profit from its own arrangement of inner achievements, separate from the more extensive venture achievements. These inner achievements are more helpful on profoundly complex activities with various degrees of endorsement and various divisions providing data.

Execution plan achievements could look like these: underlying partner data assembled, plan drafted, plan talked about and criticism integrated, last close down by all partners.

Execution plan KPIs and measurements

Your key exhibition pointers (KPIs) or different measurements uncover how well the group is achieving the execution plan. Lay out quantifiable pointers, state what they are inside the actual arrangement, and afterward track them throughout the span of the task.

Here, a quality undertaking the executives device is fundamental to prevail with estimations that range the length of a task.

5 simple tasks to make your venture execution plan

Presently you understand what requirements to go into your undertaking execution plan — yet how would you really make one and kick the execution interaction off?

We realize this interaction can appear to be overwhelming from the start, and it takes some forthright work. In any case, the cycle doesn't need to be essentially as convoluted as it appears. Follow these five simple tasks to make an execution plan that helps keep your venture and your group on target. Then, at that point, as future tasks emerge, utilize these inquiries as a layout of sorts to make a quality execution and the board plan for every one.

1) Characterize your objectives and achievements

Before you can make an arrangement for how to get where you need to go, you want to invest some energy choosing where you need to go.

Thus, before you begin working out some other piece of a venture execution or activity plan, begin by giving opportunity to the what and the where:

* What are you attempting to achieve? (Project-level objectives)

* What necessities to end up arriving at those objectives? (Project goals)

* What are the moderate advances or achievements that exhibit progress along the way toward the task's objectives? (Project achievements)

When you lay out objectives, targets, and achievements — and accomplish purchase in from key partners and venture colleagues on those objectives and achievements — you're prepared to continue to stage two.

2) Direct examination by talking, reviewing, or noticing

Research is one critical component of an effective execution plan. In many undertaking settings, this examination looks like talking or reviewing different partners, educated authorities, office pioneers, etc — gathering the data important to fabricate your execution methodology.

Here and there perception is a critical technique too: Watching what another group (or seller or outer association) does or has done on a comparable task can give significant bits of knowledge.

3) Conceptualize and delineate possible dangers

Each task has innate possible dangers. A portion of these can be predicted, while others appear to appear suddenly. Accept the pandemic as one illustration of the last class. Indeed, organizations ought to have business congruity and fiasco the board strategies set up, yet few — if any — organizations had a substantial strategy arranged for a worldwide pandemic.

Thus, there are takes a chance with you can't anticipate and would never foresee. Yet, there are a lot of dangers that, with a smidgen of conceptualizing and arranging, ought to be not difficult to find. These are the ones you really want to focus as you play out a gamble evaluation.

Map out the known dangers, alongside likely effects and relief techniques for every one. A few dangers are very much avoidable insofar as you make fitting gamble the executives moves. Others may not be totally preventable, yet having an arrangement set up will significantly decrease their effect.

4) Appoint and designate fundamental undertakings

Each great execution plan will incorporate a work plan or activity plan that rundowns out the errands inside the venture to a specific degree of granularity. These undertakings ultimately get connected to a schedule or timetable or some likeness thereof, frequently inside project arranging programming suites.

Regardless of what strategy or stage you're utilizing, at this stage, you really want to delineate or plan these errands. As a piece of this step, ensure you dole out and designate undertakings to explicit assets (or, at least, explicit divisions or work gatherings).

This step is critical to effective undertaking execution, as it appoints liability and responsibility for each errand remembered for the arrangement, carrying lucidity to who's doing what and when.

5) Settle your arrangement and distribute assets

Next up is apportioning assets. You previously allocated undertakings to individuals (or offices) in the past step, so what do we mean here that is any unique?

Set forth plainly, there's a contrast between writing down that "Sam will deal with task 35" (relegating undertakings) and really ensuring that Sam has the ability to deal with task 35 (distributing assets).

In sync 4, all you truly did was figure out who's doing what. Presently, during asset portion, you ensure that your task plan is reachable. Asset portion implies relegating assignments to assets that are really accessible. All in all, you want to ensure task 35 doesn't arrive in front of Sam that very day as 10 different undertakings.

Last, when all the other things about your arrangement has been created, checked, and supported, now is the right time to conclude the arrangement. Generally, this includes conveying the finished arrangement for a last round of endorsements.

When endorsed, the venture execution plan turns into a solitary wellspring of truth for the group and different partners. So make a point to store the arrangement in a focal, open area.

○ **Tracking and Measuring Results**

Powerful objective setting is imperative inside associations, however defining those objectives is just the initial step to progress. To augment the advantages of objective setting, you should consistently track and measure progress toward those objectives, which we'll examine in this article.

We likewise present procedures and devices for objective following, make sense of how for measure achievement, and guide you in adjusting your objectives as needed.

If you're searching for a useful asset to track and quantify every one of your objectives in a single spot, you can open a free preliminary with Wrike today.

The significance of following and estimating objectives.

Following and estimating objectives is vital on the grounds that it:

* Guarantees arrangement with and center around authoritative needs

* Uncovers progress and distinguishes barriers

* Assists you with making ideal acclimations to objectives or techniques on a case by case basis

* Improves responsibility and inspiration among colleagues

* Gives significant information to assessing execution and illuminating future objective setting

Objective tracker: Picking the right device for your association.

You really want the right objective following instrument to screen progress toward your objectives. While picking an objective global positioning framework, think about the accompanying elements:

* Coordination with existing frameworks: A decent following device ought to effectively incorporate with your association's current undertaking the executives, correspondence, and detailing instruments.

* Adaptability: It ought to be adequately adjustable to oblige your association's remarkable objectives, targets, and execution markers.

* Versatility: As your association develops, your objective following instrument ought to have the option to scale with you.

* Convenience: An easy to understand interface lets colleagues rapidly and effectively access and update objective data to remain focused.

* Announcing capacities: Objective following requires detailing highlights that let you break

down progress, distinguish patterns, and settle on choices in light of sound information.

Whether you favor an objective following application or a work the board stage, you'll need to find one that matches the requirements of your group and association.

Objective following methods

A few methods can be utilized to follow progress toward objectives. In this part, you'll figure out how to utilize gatherings, reports, and the sky is the limit from there.

Progress gatherings

Normal advancement gatherings allow colleagues an opportunity to examine objective advancement, share updates, and address difficulties or road obstructions. These gatherings can be held everyday, week by week, fortnightly, or month to month, contingent upon the idea of your objectives and the speed of your association. Urge your group to share their contemplations unreservedly during these gatherings to advance a culture of shared responsibility.

Dashboard detailing

Dashboards give a visual portrayal of objective advancement and can be an incredible method for following KPIs and other significant measurements. Colleagues can utilize dashboard answering to rapidly survey progress and recognize regions that require consideration. You could in fact tweak your dashboards to show applicable data for various divisions, groups, or people.

Standard registrations

One-in one registrations between colleagues and their bosses can assist with keeping individual objectives on target. Registrations allow you an opportunity to survey progress, give criticism, and examine any issues in a less open setting.

Plan registrations without fail to receive the most reward from them.

Achievements and cutoff times

Separating objectives into more modest achievements with explicit cutoff times keeps up with energy. By setting and checking achievements, groups can keep fixed on accomplishing their objectives while likewise commending those terrifically significant successes en route.

Mechanized following

Mechanized following programming does considerably more than objective tracker applications can. The previous can save you time checking progress toward objectives and give constant updates. These instruments can likewise assist you with spotting bottlenecks, smooth out work processes, oversee assignments, and fulfill time constraints.

143

Execution surveys

By integrating objective following into normal execution surveys, you can all the more likely evaluate a singular's advancement toward their objectives and cultivate a culture of ceaseless improvement and advancement.

The right mix of these objective following strategies can assist your association with keeping up with center, improve responsibility, and accomplish its targets.

Step by step instructions to quantify achievement

In this way, presently you know how to follow your objectives in principle. Be that as it may, how might you guarantee they're really effective? Here are a hints and achievement measurements to consider while estimating objective achievement.

* Achievement models: Lay out clear and quantifiable achievement rules for every objective, for example, explicit KPIs, monetary measurements, client related measurements, or different measures.

* Quantitative measurements: These are evenhanded, mathematical measurements, for example, income development, cost decrease, portion of the overall industry, or client obtaining. Quantitative measurements can be followed over the long run to survey the outcome of your objectives.

* Subjective measurements: These are abstract measurements, like consumer loyalty, worker resolve, or enhancements in inward cycles. Subjective measurements can be estimated through studies, meetings, or center gatherings.

* Driving and trailing results: Proactive factors are proactive measures that anticipate future execution, for example, potential customers or

site traffic. In the mean time, trailing results are responsive measures that reflect past execution, like income or benefit. By following both driving and trailing results, you'll get a full image of your objective achievement.

* Progress surveys: Constantly evaluate progress toward your objectives and contrast it with your prosperity models. Like that, you can rapidly recognize expected regions for development and change your techniques on a case by case basis.

* Influence: Dissect the more extensive effect of accomplishing your objectives on your association's general execution, development, and improvement.

Changing your objectives

As you track and measure your objectives, you might have to change them now and again. Here are a few ways to change your objectives on a case by case basis.

* Be adaptable: Comprehend that conditions and needs might change, expecting you to in like manner change your objectives.

* Look for criticism: Request normal input from colleagues, friends, and managers to recognize regions for development and make expected acclimations to your objectives.

* Reevaluate needs: Intermittently rethink your association's needs to guarantee that your objectives stay lined up with your essential goals.

* Refine objectives in light of information: Utilize the information assembled through your objective following endeavors to recognize patterns, examples, and regions for development. Refine your objectives and methodologies in view of these.

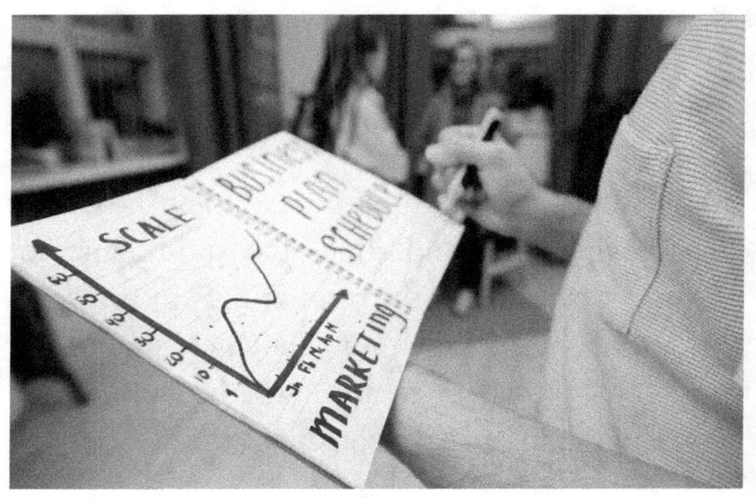
SCALE
BUSINESS
PLAN
SCHEDULE
FINAN
MARKETing

CONCLUSION

○ **Summarizing Key Takeaways**

1.Effortlessness is Power: The 1-Page Showcasing Plan underlines the significance of straightforwardness in promoting. In a world immersed with data, a succinct and clear arrangement can slice through the commotion and catch your crowd's consideration really.

Clear Business Objectives: Characterizing clear and quantifiable business objectives is the underpinning of any fruitful advertising plan. Your goals ought to direct your advertising system.

2.Make a Convincing Message: Your message is your image's voice. Making a convincing offer and brand story is fundamental to sincerely interface with your ideal interest group.

Pick the Right Channels: Select showcasing channels that line up with your crowd.

Understanding where your crowd invests their energy is vital for successful correspondence.

3.Make Your 1-Page Plan: Fabricate a compact showcasing plan that incorporates key parts like your ideal interest group, one of a kind selling suggestion, channels, and spending plan contemplations. Layouts and models can assist with smoothing out this interaction.

Execution is Vital: A significant arrangement is just powerful in the event that you execute it. Do whatever it may take to carry out your showcasing system, measure results, and be prepared to adjust depending on the situation.

4.Gain from Contextual analyses: Genuine contextual investigations give important bits of knowledge into fruitful 1-Page Advertising Plans. Comprehend how others have applied these standards to accomplish outstanding outcomes.

Investigate Difficulties: Address normal difficulties, for example, spending plan requirements and changing economic situations. Be ready to adjust and track down effective fixes.

Scale for Long haul Achievement: As your business develops, scale your promoting endeavors while keeping up with consistency in your informing and marking.

5.Pragmatic Assets: The book gives formats, worksheets, and extra assets to help you make and refine your 1-Page Showcasing Plan.

In reality as we know it where capacities to focus are short, and rivalry is wild, effortlessness and lucidity in your advertising approach are vital. The 1-Page Promoting Plan is a down to earth manual for fostering a strong, versatile showcasing procedure that can drive your business forward. It's a guide to accomplishing your objectives in a consistently developing showcasing scene.